Nine Days To

REDISCOVER
THE JOY OF PRAYER

Nine Days To

REDISCOVER
THE JOY OF PRAYER

JACQUES PHILIPPE

Scepter

Nine Days for . . .

Collection edited by Timothée Berthon

The "Nine Days for" collection offers a guided retreat to be lived at home or on vacation, in the subway or on the train . . . for people who have little time but wish to devote ten minutes a day to spiritual growth.

Each book in the collection offers nine days of inspiring meditations that surround a specific theme for advancement in the spiritual life. Each serves as both a school of prayer and an authentic tool of self-transformation.

Two meditations are offered for each day. One can be experienced in the morning and the other at any opportune moment during the day or evening.

The journey includes reflection exercises, the Word of God, a meditation from a saint or another great spiritual author, and a resolution— all geared to help the participant dive into an authentic spiritual experience.

These journeys are offered both in pamphlet and audio CD form.

JACQUES PHILIPPE

Published by Scepter Publishers, Inc.
info@scepterpublishers.org
www.scepterpublishers.org
800-322-8773
New York

All rights reserved.

Text and cover design by Rose Design

Cover image: Shutterstock.com

Library of Congress Cataloging-in-Publication Data

Names: Philippe, Jacques, 1947- author.
Title: Nine days to rediscover the joy of prayer / Jacques Philippe.
Other titles: 9 jours pour retrouver la joie de prier. English
Description: New York : Scepter Publishers, 2019.
Identifiers: LCCN 2018058077 (print) | LCCN 2018059686 (ebook) | ISBN
   9781594173363 (eBook) | ISBN 9781594173356 (pbk. : alk. paper)
Subjects: LCSH: Prayer--Catholic Church--Meditations.
Classification: LCC BV210.3 (ebook) | LCC BV210.3 .P459513 2019 (print)
| DDC
   248.3/2--dc23
LC record available at https://lccn.loc.gov/2018058077

PB ISBN: 9781594173356   eBook ISBN: 9781594173363

Printed in the United States of America

Contents

First Day

RESPONDING TO A CALL

Daily Meditation

INTRODUCTION

To begin our retreat, we consider an essential aspect of prayer: that prayer is a response to a call.

INVITATION TO CONTEMPLATION

First of all, I am taking a moment to contemplate. I seat myself, present to the current moment, relaxed. I am breathing, calmly.

With the eyes of faith, I make myself attentive to God's presence, which resides in my heart. I thank him and entrust myself to his love.

SIGN OF THE CROSS

I pray in the name of the Father, and of the Son, and of the Holy Spirit. Amen.

PRAYER TO THE HOLY SPIRIT

Holy Spirit, ignite in my heart a new burning for you.

THE WORD OF GOD

In chapter twenty-one of the Gospel of Luke, Christ tells us: "Pray without ceasing!"

MEDITATION FROM FR. JACQUES PHILIPPE

The first thing that should motivate us and encourage us to enter into a life of prayer is that God himself invites us. Man seeks God, but God seeks man far more. God calls us to pray to him, because, since the beginning—and way more than we can imagine it—he ardently desires to enter into communion with us.

The most solid foundation for a life of prayer isn't our own efforts, our own personal initiatives, or our desires (they have their place, but can sometimes be insufficient). The most solid foundation for a life of prayer is God's calling.

We don't pray because we desire God, or because we expect particular advantages from our prayer life, but, first and foremost, we pray because God asks us to. And, in so asking, God knows what he's doing. His project infinitely surpasses what we can see, desire, or imagine. There is, in prayer, a mystery that absolutely surpasses us. The engine of prayer life is faith, in the sense of confident obedience to what God suggests to us. We are unable to imagine the immense positive repercussions of this humble and trusting response to God's call, like Abraham, who undertook a journey without knowing where he was going but who became the father of many.

If we pray because of the advantages that we count on obtaining from prayer, we run the risk of being discouraged someday. These advantages are neither immediate nor measurable. If we pray with a humble attitude of submission to God's Word, we will always have the grace of perseverance.

PRAYER

Lord, you never stop calling us to follow you and to love you. Grant that we may hear your call this day, encounter you in prayer, and respond to you generously. We ask you this through the intercession of Mary.

Hail Mary, full of grace, the Lord is with thee. Blessed art thou among women, and blessed is the fruit of thy womb, Jesus. Holy Mary, Mother of God, pray for us sinners, now and at the hour of our death. Amen.

DAILY RESOLUTION

Today , I will think as often as possible how God loves me, and how happy he is when I take a few moments out of my activities to think of him and confide in him.

THE LIGHT OF THE SAINTS

"I want to be faithful, very faithful to prayer every day, in spite of all the dryness, boredom, or distaste that I may encounter . . . in spite of the unpleasant, discouraging, threatening things the Devil may tell me! . . . On days of trouble and torment, I will tell myself: God wants this, my vocation requires this, and that's enough for me! I will do the prayer, I will keep at it for the whole time I have been told to, I will do the prayer as well as I can, and when it is time to stop, I will say to God boldly: 'My God, I haven't prayed, I haven't worked, I've done nothing, but I've obeyed you. I've suffered a lot, but I've shown you that I love you and want to love you."

—Marthe Robin[1]

"I expect nothing more than that you wait for me."

—Jesus to Sister Mary of the Trinity

---

1. Marthe Robin, as quoted in Jacques Philippe, *Thirsting for Prayer* (New York, N.Y.: Scepter, 2014), p. 8.

GUIDE FOR A SECOND PRAYER TIME

Man seeks God, but God seeks man much more. I am meditating by repeating Jesus' words several times: *"You did not choose me, but I chose you and appointed you that you should go and bear fruit"* (Jn 15:16).

I contemplate God's desire to enter into a relationship with each one of his children, the desire that he has to communicate himself to us so as to be our supreme Good.

I keep myself in God's gaze; I have confidence in his love, and I let myself be drawn in by him.

Second Day

PUTTING GOD FIRST

Daily Meditation

INTRODUCTION

During this second day of our retreat, we're trying to make a little more progress in prayer. When we pray, God can take center place in our lives.

INVITATION TO CONTEMPLATION

To enter into a state of prayerfulness, I take a moment to recollect myself. I settle in comfortably, remaining upright, arms uncrossed, feet resting flatly against the ground.

I close my eyes. I welcome the Lord's presence; I thank him for the faithfulness of his love.

SIGN OF THE CROSS

I pray in the name of the Father, and of the Son, and of the Holy Spirit. Amen.

Prayer to the Holy Spirit

Holy Spirit, you, the interior Master, open my heart to receive your Word in this day.

The Word of God

"Seek first his kingdom and his righteousness, and all these things shall be yours as well" (Mt 6:33).

MEDITATION FROM FR. JACQUES PHILIPPE

Human existence only finds its fullness, equilibrium, and beauty when God is at its center. "Serve God first!" St. Joan of Arc said. Faithfulness to prayer allows us to guarantee, in a concrete, effective way, the primacy of God. Without it, the priority given to God risks merely being a good intention, or even an illusion.

Those who do not pray put their egos, subtly but certainly, at the center of their lives, instead of the living person of God. They will be scattered by a multitude of desires, demands, and fears. Those who pray, on the other hand, even if they must confront the weight of ego, the forces that make us turn in on ourselves, the egoism that exists in all of us, will be making a movement toward re-centering away from self and toward God, which little by little will let God take (or retake) his proper place in their lives: the central place. In this way they will find the unity and coherence of their lives. "He who does not gather with me scatters" Jesus says in the Gospel of Luke (Lk 11:23). When God is at the center, everything falls into its right place.

Giving God absolute primacy in relation to all other things (work, human relationships, etc.) is the only way to establish a right relation with things, a true investment and holy distance that lets us keep interior freedom and unity in our lives. Otherwise, we fall into indifference, either negligence or attachment, an invasion, or a scattering, of useless worries.

Prayer

Lord, you invite me to seek first the kingdom of heaven. Today I want to learn to pray; teach me to recognize you, to call on you, to live with you. Help me to decide to pray each day. I ask you this through the intercession of Mary, your mother.

Hail Mary, full of grace, the Lord is with thee. Blessed art thou among women, and blessed is the fruit of thy womb, Jesus. Holy Mary, Mother of God, pray for us sinners, now and at the hour of our death. Amen.

Daily Resolution

This evening, before going to bed, I will take five minutes to thank God for being the true center of my life. I will give back to him everything that made up this day: the good that I've accomplished to give thanks to him, the difficulties that I've encountered to ask for his help, my faults and imperfections to ask him for forgiveness. In this way, everything that made up my day will find its fulfillment in God. And I will go to sleep in peace, confident in his mercy.

THE LIGHT OF THE SAINTS

"It would be wrong to think that ordinary Christians can be content with a shallow prayer that is unable to fill their whole life. Especially in the face of the many trials to which today's world subjects faith, they would be not only mediocre Christians but 'Christians at risk.'"[1]

—St. John Paul II

"Our life is worth what our prayer is worth."[2]

—Marthe Robin

---

1. John Paul II, Apostolic Letter *Novo millennio ineunte* (January 6, 2001), 34. Vatican website: *www.vatican.va.*

2. Marthe Robin, as quoted in Jacques Philippe, *Thirsting for Prayer* (New York, N.Y.: Scepter, 2014), p. 1.

GUIDE FOR A SECOND PRAYER TIME

When God is at the center, everything finds its right place.

During my time of personal prayer, in silence, I slowly read the first four verses of Psalm 63 several times over:

> "O God, thou art my God, I seek thee,
>   my soul thirsts for thee;
> my flesh faints for thee,
>   as in a dry and weary land where no water is.
> So I have looked upon thee in the sanctuary,
>   beholding thy power and glory.
> Because thy steadfast love is better than life,
>   my lips will praise thee.
> So I will bless thee as long as I live;
>   I will lift up my hands and call on thy name."

Then I will choose a single, brief phrase and I will repeat it in my heart over the course of several minutes with my eyes closed, letting it penetrate me.

Third Day

PRAYING FREELY

Daily Meditation

INTRODUCTION

On this third day of our retreat, we are asking the Lord to continue his work during this time that we spend with him each day. We are meditating today on an essential aspect of prayer: its freeness.

INVITATION TO CONTEMPLATION

Lord, I make myself available to your presence. I give you everything that inhabits my heart; I raise my eyes toward you, and I welcome your love.

SIGN OF THE CROSS

I pray in the name of the Father, and of the Son, and of the Holy Spirit. Amen.

PRAYER TO THE HOLY SPIRIT

Holy Spirit, make my heart disposed to welcome your light.

THE WORD OF GOD

During the Last Supper that Jesus shared with his disciples, he told them "No longer do I call you servants . . . but I have called you friends" (Jn 15:15).

MEDITATION FROM FR. JACQUES PHILIPPE

Faithfulness to prayer is precious because it helps us to preserve the aspect of freeness in our lives. Praying means sacrificing one's time for God. At its base, it's about freely giving God our love.

This sense of freeness is menaced by today's attitude where everything is thought of in terms of price, efficiency, and performance. True love cannot be fit into the category of usefulness. The Gospel of Mark, when he recounts the establishment of the twelve, tells us that Jesus chose them first of all "to be with him" (Mk 3:14). And then only after that to share in his work: to preach, drive out demons, etc. We are not only servants; we are called to be friends, in a life of shared intimacy, beyond all utilitarianism.

To pray is to spend time freely with God, for the joy of being together. It is to love, because giving one's time means giving one's life. Love doesn't consist first of doing something for another, but in being present for him or her. Prayer teaches us to be present to God, with a simple, loving attention.

The marvel is that, in learning to be present to God alone, we learn at the same time to be present to others. With people who have lived a long life of prayer, we perceive the quality of attention, of presence, of listening, and of availability that is often not possible with people whose lives are taken up with activities. A certain delicacy is born of prayer: a respect, an attention that is a precious gift for those whom we encounter on our way.

There is no more beautiful nor more effective school for attention to our neighbors than perseverance in prayer.

PRAYER

Thank you, Lord, for calling us to share in your life, for making us your friends. Help us to enter into this free relationship with you and with our neighbors. We ask you this through the intercession of Mary, your mother.

Hail Mary, full of grace, the Lord is with thee. Blessed art thou among women, and blessed is the fruit of thy womb, Jesus. Holy Mary, Mother of God, pray for us sinners, now and at the hour of our death. Amen.

DAILY RESOLUTION

Today, I will spend free time with Jesus. During this period, I will remain in silence for some time and I will hear Jesus say to me: "I no longer call you servant, but friend." I will let myself be touched by these words, which come to join me in the intimacy of my relationship with him and which invite me to live no longer as a servant, but as a friend of Jesus. "I no longer call you servant, but friend."

THE LIGHT OF THE SAINTS

"It's easier to find laborers to work than children to play with."

—Jesus to Sister Mary of the Trinity

"[God] has no need of our works, but only of our *love*."[1]

—St. Thérèse of Lisieux

1. Thérèse of Lisieux, *General Correspondence Volume II*, trans. John Clarke, OCD (Washington, D.C.: ICS Publications, 1988), p. 299.

GUIDE FOR A SECOND PRAYER TIME

Prayer teaches us to be present to God, with a simple, loving attention.

I slowly read this passage from the Gospel of St. Luke:

"Now as they went on their way, he entered a village; and a woman named Martha received him into her house. And she had a sister called Mary, who sat at the Lord's feet and listened to his teaching. But Martha was distracted with much serving; and she went to him and said, 'Lord, do you not care that my sister has left me to serve alone? Tell her then to help me.' But the Lord answered her, 'Martha, Martha, you are anxious and troubled about many things; one thing is needful. Mary has chosen the good portion, which shall not be taken away from her'" (Lk 10: 38–42).

I softly repeat the following phrase several times: "Mary sat at the Lord's feet and listened to his teaching." I let this simple phrase penetrate my heart, and I make its attitude my own: I, too, remain like Mary, peaceably seated at the feet of the Lord, welcoming his presence and listening to his Word.

Fourth Day

LIVING HEAVEN ON EARTH

Daily Meditation

INTRODUCTION

Today we meditate on the "already there" of the kingdom. In prayer, we are living a foretaste of heaven, which makes us anticipate the kingdom.

INVITATION TO CONTEMPLATION

At the beginning of my prayer, I take a moment to recollect myself. I use my breath to help me with that. I breathe deeply . . . and exhale. I do it again until the tension that is within me lets go, and a relaxation and availability in me takes hold. I turn myself to the Lord; I thank him for being there, present, for me.

SIGN OF THE CROSS

I pray in the name of the Father, and of the Son, and of the Holy Spirit. Amen.

PRAYER TO THE HOLY SPIRIT

Holy Spirit, divine host of my soul, teach me to contemplate the realities of on high.

THE WORD OF GOD

"Fear not, little flock, for it is your Father's good pleasure to give you the kingdom" (Lk 12:32).

MEDITATION FROM FR. JACQUES PHILIPPE

Prayer makes us anticipate heaven. It lets us glimpse and savor a happiness that isn't of this world, one that nothing here below offers us, this happiness from God that we are destined for and for which we were created.

We go through combats, suffering, and arid periods in prayer life. But if we persevere faithfully, from time to time we taste an indescribable happiness, a peace and reassurance that are a foretaste of paradise.

"You will see heaven opened," Jesus promised us (Jn 1:51).

All of this is to say that, in prayer, mankind learns even from this earth what his activity and joy will be for all eternity: to be enraptured with divine beauty and the glory of the kingdom. We learn to do what we were created for. We put the most beautiful and profound faculties that we possess as human beings into action: the faculties of adoration, admiration, praise, and thanksgiving. We rediscover the heart and viewpoint of a child, marveling at the Beauty above all beauty.

Praying also means, then, that we fulfill ourselves as human persons, according to the most profound potential of our nature and the most secret aspirations of our hearts. We don't live through this feeling every day, of course, but everyone who embarks with faithfulness and good will on the path of prayer will experience something of it, at least in certain moments of grace. Especially today: there is so much ugliness, evil, and heaviness in our world that God, who is faithful and wants to revive our hope, doesn't miss the opportunity to reveal the treasures of his kingdom to his children.

St. John of the Cross affirmed in the sixteenth century: "The Lord has always revealed to mortals the treasures of his wisdom and his spirit, but now that the face of evil bares itself more and more, so does the Lord bare his treasures more."[1]

PRAYER

Lord, you made us for happiness even from this earth and we thank you for it. Teach us to live the celestial realities starting today; train our vision to discern your presence in our lives, awaken our intelligence to your divine mysteries, and fortify our wills so that all our acts be those of praise to your glory. We ask you this through Mary's hands.

Hail Mary, full of grace, the Lord is with thee. Blessed art thou among women, and blessed is the fruit of thy womb, Jesus. Holy Mary, Mother

1. John of the Cross, *The Collected Works of St. John of the Cross* (Washington, D.C.: ICS Publications, 1991). Kindle.

of God, pray for us sinners, now and at the hour of our death. Amen.

Daily Resolution

All day long I will be attentive to God's presence, to him who ceaselessly accompanies me. I will try to be aware of what the Lord wants to teach me about his kingdom today.

The Light of the Saints

"To taste in a certain way in our heart, to experience in our spirit, the force of the divine presence and the sweetness of the glory above, not only after death, but even in this mortal life."

> —Excerpt from the first rule of the Order of the Brothers of Our Lady of Mount Carmel, founded in the Holy Land in the twelfth century.

"Rouse yourselves, my sisters, and since some foretaste of heaven may be had on earth, beg our Lord to give us grace not to miss it through our own fault. Ask Him to show us where to find it—ask Him to give us strength of soul to dig until we find this hidden treasure, which lies buried within our hearts."[2]

—St. Teresa of Ávila

"Prayer is a foretaste of heaven, and overflow of paradise. It never leaves us without sweetness. It is like honey descending into the soul and sweetening everything."[3]

—St. John Vianney

---

2. Teresa of Jesus, *The Interior Castle or The Mansions,* trans. The Benedictines of Stanbrook (New York: Benziger Brothers, 2011), pp. 92–93.

3. John Vianney, *The Little Catechism of the Curé of Ars* (Charlotte, N.C.: TAN Books, 2015), p. 29

GUIDE FOR A SECOND PRAYER TIME

To pray is to regain the heart of a child and marvel at the beauty of God.

I softly read the following passages from Scripture. I choose a verse, repeat it slowly, and let it sink in.

"Preserve me, O God, for in thee I take refuge.
  I say to the Lord, 'Thou art my Lord;
  I have no good apart from thee.'
The Lord is my chosen portion and my cup;
  thou holdest my lot.
The lines have fallen for me in pleasant places;
  yea, I have a goodly heritage."
  (Ps 16:1–2, 5–6)

"Behold, you are beautiful, my beloved,
  truly lovely." (Song 1:16)

"You are the fairest of the sons of men;
  grace is poured upon your lips;
  therefore God has blessed you for ever."
  (Ps 45:2)

Fifth Day

PRAYER MAKES ME KNOW GOD

Daily Meditation

INTRODUCTION

We continue our retreat, seized with this desire to find or to re-encounter the joy of prayer. Today, we are going to see how prayer draws us little by little into a real knowledge of God.

INVITATION TO CONTEMPLATION

To begin my prayer, I seat myself comfortably and I relax. I breathe calmly, and—with an attitude of faith—I make myself attentive to God's presence, which resides in my heart. I thank him, and I trust in his love.

SIGN OF THE CROSS

I trace over my body the beautiful Sign of the Cross and begin my prayer in the name of the Father, and of the Son, and of the Holy Spirit. Amen.

Prayer to the Holy Spirit

We invoke you, Holy Spirit, in this day, you who made us your sons and daughters. Show us the true face of the Father, and make us know the Son in spirit and in truth.

The Word of God

"For you did not receive the spirit of slavery to fall back into fear, but you have received the spirit of sonship. When we cry, 'Abba! Father!' it is the Spirit himself bearing witness with our spirit that we are children of God" (Rm 8:15–16).

Meditation from Fr. Jacques Philippe

Prayer introduces us little by little into a true knowledge of God. Not an abstract God, far off, Voltaire's "great watchmaker," or the God of philosophers and wise men. Nor even a cold, cerebral, theological one, but the personal God, living and true, the God of Abraham, Isaac, and Jacob, the Father of our Lord Jesus Christ—God who spoke to our hearts, to use Pascal's expression. Not a God about whom we are contented merely to know some received ideas from our education or our culture, less still a God who is the product of our psychological projections, but the true God.

Prayer permits us to go from our ideas about God, from our representations (always either wrong or too narrow) to an experience of God. And that's very different.

The principal object of God's personal revelation, an essential fruit of prayer, is to know him as a father: God as the boundless source of life, as the Origin, as an inexhaustible gift, as generosity, and God as kindness, tenderness, and infinite mercy.

The beautiful passage from the book of Jeremiah, which announces the New Covenant, finishes with these words:

"But this is the covenant which I will make with the house of Israel after those days, says the Lord: I will put my law within them, and I will write it upon their hearts; and I will be their God, and they shall be my people. And no longer shall each man teach his neighbor and each his brother, saying, 'Know the Lord,' for they shall all know me, from the least of them to the greatest" (Jer 31:33–34).

God is known in his grandeur, his transcendence, his majesty, and his infinite power, but at the same time in his tenderness, his closeness, his sweetness, his inexhaustible mercy. This understanding is not knowledge, but an experience lived with one's whole being.

PRAYER

You made us for you, Lord, and our hearts are without rest so long as they don't truly know you, so long as they don't rest in you. Teach us to know you; reveal yourself to us, Lord; make us experience your fatherly love. We ask this through the intercession of Mary.

Hail Mary, full of Grace, the Lord is with thee. Blessed art thou among women, and blessed is the fruit of thy womb, Jesus. Holy Mary, Mother of God, pray for us sinners, now and at the hour of our death. Amen.

Daily Resolution

I take time to read the Word of God from the liturgy of the day. I contemplate the face of God that this passage from the Word reveals to me. I meditate on it and keep it in my heart.

The Light of the Saints

"To converse with You, O Lord, is the delight of my heart. In You I find everything that my heart could desire. Here your light illuminates my mind, enabling it to know You more and more deeply."[1]

—St. Faustina

"It is so sweet to call God our Father!"[2]

—St. Thérèse of Lisieux

1. Maria Faustina Kowalska, *Diary of Saint Maria Faustina Kowalska: Divine Mercy in My Soul* (Stockbridge, MA: Marian Press, 2014), 1692.

2. Céline Martin, *My Sister Saint Thérèse* (Charlotte, N.C.: TAN Books, 1997). Kindle.

GUIDE FOR A SECOND PRAYER TIME

Prayer makes us know God as a father, as kindness, tenderness, and infinite mercy. I read several times, slowly, the verses of the following Psalm. I choose one, repeat it slowly, and let it sink in.

> "[He] who forgives all your iniquity,
>   who heals all your diseases,
>
> who redeems your life from the Pit,
>   who crowns you with steadfast love
>   and mercy,
>
> who satisfies you with good as long as you live
>   so that your youth is renewed like the
>   eagle's." (Ps 103:3–5)

> "As a father pities his children,
>   so the Lord pities those who fear him.
>
> For he knows our frame;
>   he remembers that we are dust."
>   (Ps 103:13–14)

Sixth Day

DISCOVERING MY PROFOUND IDENTITY

Daily Meditation

INTRODUCTION

On this sixth day of retreat, we meditate on one of the fruits of prayer: self-knowledge. Mankind does not truly know itself without the light of God.

INVITATION TO CONTEMPLATION

To prepare myself for prayer, I create interior silence. I progressively leave aside the thoughts that assail me, the things I have to do, new ideas, worries . . . to center myself on Christ. I enter little by little into a living silence. And if a thought comes to distract me, as soon as I perceive it, I carefully re-center my attention on Christ who is there, present, in me.

SIGN OF THE CROSS

I pray in the name of the Father, and of the Son, and of the Holy Spirit. Amen.

PRAYER TO THE HOLY SPIRIT

Holy Spirit, send down on us this day a ray of your light. May our lives be illuminated by it.

THE WORD OF GOD

"Thou art my beloved Son; with thee I am well pleased" (Lk 3:22).

MEDITATION FROM FR. JACQUES PHILIPPE

Mankind can only truly know itself with the light of God. All that we can know of ourselves through human means (life experiences, psychology, social sciences) are not to be denigrated, of course. But those things give us a limited and partial knowledge of our being. We only have access to our profound identity through the light of God, in the regard that God has on us as the Father in heaven.

This knowledge has a negative aspect, but it is one that leads to something positive. The negative aspect concerns our sin, our profound misery. We don't really recognize it but in the light of God. Faced with him, lies are no longer possible; there's no escaping, no justification, no more masks to cling to. We are obliged to recognize who we are, with our wounds, our weaknesses, our inconsistencies, our egoism, our hardness of heart, our secret complicities with evil, etc.

Happily, God is tender and merciful, and this light that is shed on us is done so progressively, as we are able to handle it. God only shows us our sin while simultaneously revealing his forgiveness and his mercy. We discover the sadness of our sinful condition, but also our absolute poverty as creatures.

This step toward truth is necessary: there is no healing without knowledge of the sickness. Only the truth makes us free. Fortunately, things do not stop there. They lead on to something still more profound and infinitely beautiful: beyond our sins and our misery, the discovery of our condition as children of God. God loves us just as we are, with an absolutely unconditional love, and it's this love that forms our deepest identity.

More deep and essential than our human limits and the evil that affects us, there is at our base an intact and pure core, our identity as sons and daughters of God.

PRAYER

Lord, in this day, we ask of you the grace of humility to welcome without fear the light that you want to give us about ourselves. We wish to advance with you on this path of truth and freedom. Thank you for your tenderness and your mercy toward us.

Hail Mary, full of grace, the Lord is with thee. Blessed art thou among women, and blessed is the fruit of thy womb, Jesus. Holy Mary, Mother of God, pray for us sinners, now and at the hour of our death. Amen.

Daily Resolution

Today and only for today, I will try to welcome my own errors, the critiques of those around me, the vexations of my day with sweetness and humility. Like Therese of Lisieux, I will learn to rejoice in the weaknesses that I discover within myself; I will not try to hide them or to deny them, but with all that I am, I will throw myself confidently into the arms of the Father.

The Light of the Saints

"At that moment, a ray of light illumined my soul, and I saw the whole abyss of my misery. In the same moment I nestled close to the most Sacred Heart of Jesus with so much trust that even if I had the sins of all the damned weighing on my conscience, I would not have doubted God's mercy but, with a heart crushed to dust, I would have thrown myself into the abyss of Your mercy."[1]

—St. Faustina

1. Maria Faustina Kowalska, 1318.

GUIDE FOR A SECOND PRAYER TIME

God loves us just as we are, with an absolutely unconditional love, and it's this love that makes up our deepest identity.

I meditate on the words: "Thou art my beloved Son; with thee I am well pleased." I am the son of the Father. Such is the word that the Father pronounced on me. Beyond my weaknesses and my failures, such is my true identity. During my prayer time, I let these words descend on me. I let myself be healed of all the accusations and faults that I carry within, and I welcome God's mercy.

Seventh Day

PRAYER MAKES ME CAPABLE OF LOVING MY NEIGHBOR

Daily Meditation

INTRODUCTION

Today we meditate on one of the most beautiful fruits of prayer: love of neighbor. Prayer makes love of my neighbors grow in me.

INVITATION TO CONTEMPLATION

I prepare myself for an encounter with the Lord by taking time to relax. Being relaxed makes me more available. For that, I seat myself comfortably; I loosen my shoulders; I make note of the tension in my body; I breathe. And I find peace in leaving everything that occupies me to God and his providence.

SIGN OF THE CROSS

I pray in the name of the Father, and of the Son, and of the Holy Spirit. Amen.

Prayer to the Holy Spirit

Holy Spirit, fill my heart with your love so that I am always more available to the needs of those around me.

The Word of God

"'You shall love the Lord your God with all your heart, and with all your soul, and with all your mind, and with all your strength.' The second is this, 'You shall love your neighbor as yourself.' There is no other commandment greater than these" (Mk 12:30–31).

MEDITATION FROM FR. JACQUES PHILIPPE

One of the most beautiful fruits of prayer (and a criterion for discernment of the authenticity of prayer) is growth in love of others. If our prayer is true, it makes us closer to God, unifying us with him and making us perceive and share the infinite love that he has for each one of his creatures. Prayer expands and softens the heart. Where prayer is lacking, on the contrary, hearts are hardened and love freezes over.

This is what St. John of the Cross writes:

> "It's an evident truth that compassion for others grows so much more as the soul unites itself more to God out of love; for, the more it loves, the more it desires that this same God be loved and honored by all. And the more it has this desire, the more it works, as much in prayer as by all the other necessary means that are possible.
>
> And in those who are thus possessed by God, the fervor and the force of their charity are such that they can't shrink away nor be contented with their own profit only; but rather as it seems so little to them to go to heaven alone, they seek with anguish, with a heavenly love and with exquisite diligence, to bring to heaven with them a great number of souls. And this is born of a great love that they had for God: that is the proper fruit and effect of prayer and perfect contemplation."

PRAYER

Lord, expand in me a concern for souls, the desire to pray for their salvation. Teach me to love my neighbor in the little, daily tasks. Fortify in me the spirit of service and attention to others. I place my prayer in the hands of the Holy Virgin.

Hail Mary, full of grace, the Lord is with thee. Blessed art thou among women, and blessed is the fruit of thy womb, Jesus. Holy Mary, Mother of God, pray for us sinners, now and at the hour of our death. Amen.

DAILY RESOLUTION

Today and only for today, I will try to seize an occasion to render joyful and disinterested service to one of those close to me.

THE LIGHT OF THE SAINTS

"Man has a beautiful office, that of praying and loving. You pray, you love—that is the happiness of man upon the earth."[1]

—St. John Vianney

"He is my master; I ask Him about everything; I speak to Him about everything. Here I obtain strength and light; here I learn everything; here I am given light on how to act toward my neighbor."[2]

—St. Faustina

"I felt *charity* enter into my soul, and the need to forget myself and to please others; since then I've been happy!"[3]

—St. Thérèse of Lisieux

---

1. John Vianney, p. 29.

2. Maria Faustina Kowalska, 704.

3. Thérèse of Lisieux, *Story of a Soul*, trans. John Clarke, OCD (Washington, D.C.: ICS Publications, 1996), p. 99.

GUIDE FOR A SECOND PRAYER TIME

Compassion for one's neighbor grows so much more as the soul unifies itself more to God out of love.

"'I was hungry and you gave me food, I was thirsty and you gave me drink, I was a stranger and you welcomed me, I was naked and you clothed me, I was sick and you visited me, I was in prison and you came to me.' Then the righteous will answer him, 'Lord, when did we see thee hungry and feed thee, or thirsty and give thee drink? And when did we see thee a stranger and welcome thee, or naked and clothe thee? And when did we see thee sick or in prison and visit thee?' And the King will answer them, 'Truly, I say to you, as you did it to one of the least of these my brethren, you did it to me'" (Mt 25:35–40).

I meditate on this text, and then I repeat several times slowly this phrase in my heart: "as you did it to one of the least of these my brethren, you did it to me." I ask Jesus this question: Who is the least of these my brethren I am especially invited to occupy myself with today, and in whom I am called to see your presence?

Eighth Day

THE MORE I PRAY, THE MORE I BECOME FREE

Daily Meditation

INTRODUCTION

Prayer is a school of freedom. The more I am faithful to prayer, the more I become free.

INVITATION TO CONTEMPLATION

I recollect myself today in addressing myself to Christ who is here, present in the most intimate part of my being:

> Jesus, Son of the Living God, have mercy on me, a poor sinner.

> Jesus, Son of the Living God, have mercy on me, a poor sinner.

> Jesus, Son of the Living God, have mercy on me, a poor sinner.

SIGN OF THE CROSS

I pray in the name of the Father, and of the Son, and of the Holy Spirit. Amen.

PRAYER TO THE HOLY SPIRIT

O heavenly King, Consoler, Spirit of Truth, you who are present everywhere and who permeates everything, treasure of good and source of life, come and live in us, purify us from all stain, and save our souls, you who are kindness.

THE WORD OF GOD

One of the scribes came up and heard them disputing with one another, and seeing that he answered them well, asked him, "Which commandment is the first of all?" Jesus answered, "The first is, 'Hear, O Israel: The Lord our God, the Lord is one'" (Mk 12:28–29).

MEDITATION FROM
FR. JACQUES PHILIPPE

Faithfulness to prayer is a path of freedom. It leads us progressively to seek in God (and to find, because "he who seeks finds," as Matthew's Gospel (7:8) assures us) the essential goods that we desire, such as: infinite and eternal love, peace, security, and happiness.

If we don't learn to receive from the hand of God these goods that are so necessary for us, we run the strong risk of looking for them elsewhere and of expecting from the things of this world (material riches, work, relationships, etc.) what they are not able to give us. Our relationships with others, for example, are sometimes deceiving because, without always realizing it, we expect from them things that they can't provide us.

Faithfulness to prayer expresses in a concrete way that we want to orient our hope for these goods toward God, in an act of faith and hope. And what we hope and expect from his mercy will be accorded to us little by little. The more

God is at the center of our lives, the more we expect everything from him and from him only, and the more our human relationships will have the chance to be well adapted and happy.

Expecting from material reality somehow what only God can accord us has a name in the Biblical tradition: idolatry. Without realizing it, we can idolize many things: people, work, acquisition of degrees, achievement of competency, success, love, pleasure, and so on. These things are good in themselves, but only on the condition that we do not ask more than what is legitimate from them. Idolatry always makes us lose a part of our freedom. Idols deceive; God, himself, never deceives us.

Experience shows that faithfulness to prayer, even if it sometimes goes through difficult periods, moments of dryness or trying times, progressively leads us to find in God a profound peace, a security, a happiness that makes us free with regard to others and to things.

PRAYER

Lord, you see my disordered attachments. I ask you pardon for the idols that have taken your place in my life, and I ask for the grace to put you at the center of my life. I put this request in the hands of Mary.

Hail Mary, full of grace, the Lord is with thee. Blessed art thou among women, and blessed is the fruit of thy womb, Jesus. Holy Mary, Mother of God, pray for us sinners, now and at the hour of our death. Amen.

DAILY RESOLUTION

What are my idols? In what or in whom have I put my profound security, my seeking for fullness? I take a moment to ask these questions of myself and to fix what has taken God's place in my life, the idol from which I am expecting security, happiness, and peace. Once identified, I ask the Lord to liberate me and to bind me ever closer to him.

THE LIGHT OF THE SAINTS

"Dare to detach yourself from everything that I am freeing you from, and use your freedom to adhere more freely and more personally to me, without anything external from you holding you back, bothering you or scattering you."

—Jesus to Sister Mary of the Trinity

"Daily prayer does not at all mean that we are virtuous; it is however a proof that we are seriously working to become so. Someone once said: we never encounter a soul that prays every day and that remains in sin."

—Marthe Robin

GUIDE FOR A SECOND PRAYER TIME

Prayer progressively leads us to find in God the essential goods that we desire.

I meditate on Psalm 131:

> "O Lord, my heart is not lifted up,
>   my eyes are not raised too high;
> I do not occupy myself with things
>   too great and too marvelous for me.
> But I have calmed and quieted my soul,
>   like a child quieted at its mother's breast;
>   like a child that is quieted is my soul.
> O Israel, hope in the Lord
>   from this time forth and for evermore."

I repeat slowly, several times, the verse: "I have calmed and quieted my soul, like a child quieted at its mother's breast," letting myself be permeated by the attitude that it describes.

Ninth Day

UNIFYING MY LIFE

Daily Meditation

INTRODUCTION

We have arrived at the conclusion of our term of nine days of prayer. Over the course of these nine days, maybe we had the experience of peace, of joy, and of renewed unity in our lives. It is prayer that creates this unity.

INVITATION TO CONTEMPLATION

I begin my prayer by assembling all my faculties. Everything that I see, my emotions, my thoughts and my memories, and my imagination—I offer them to Christ. I turn toward him, and I welcome his peace.

SIGN OF THE CROSS

I pray in the name of the Father, and of the Son, and of the Holy Spirit. Amen.

PRAYER TO THE HOLY SPIRIT

Holy Spirit, unify my heart this day so that it fears your name (see Psalm 81).

THE WORD OF GOD

"But Mary kept all these things, pondering them in her heart" (Lk 2:19).

MEDITATION FROM FR. JACQUES PHILIPPE

Over time and with faithfulness, prayer reveals itself to be a marvelous "unifying center" of our lives. In an encounter with God where we trustingly place in his fatherly hands what makes up our existence day after day, including all the various events and circumstances that we go through. Everything is "managed," little by little, integrated, wrested from chaos, from the scattering forces of incoherence.

Life then finds its profound unity. God is the one God and he who unifies our hearts, our personalities, and all our existence.

Thanks to a regular encounter with God in prayer, everything, in the end, becomes positive: our desires, our good will, our efforts, but also our poverty, our errors, our sins. Our fortunate or unfortunate circumstances, good or bad choices—everything is "summed up" in Christ and becomes grace. Everything winds up making sense and is integrated into a path of growth through love.

In the stories of Jesus' childhood, the Gospel of Luke tells us about the Virgin: "But Mary kept all these things, pondering them in her heart" (Lk 2:19). Everything that Mary lived through, the graces received, the words she heard, the events she went through, enlightening as well as sorrowful or incomprehensible, she kept them in her heart and her prayer; everything ended by making sense one day, not by virtue of some intellectual analysis, but thanks to her interior prayer.

She didn't ruminate on things in her head, but kept them in her heart, confident and praying, and everything wound up finding its pace; everything wound up being unified and simplified.

On the other hand, without faithfulness to our prayer times, our lives run the risk of remaining incoherent.

PRAYER

Lord, augment our faith. Through the good and bad circumstances of our lives, teach us always to keep the same trust, sure, in every situation, that you are present and that everything works for good for him who loves God. We place our prayer in the hands of Mary.

Hail Mary, full of grace, the Lord is with thee. Blessed art thou among women, and blessed is the fruit of thy womb, Jesus. Holy Mary, Mother of God, pray for us sinners, now and at the hour of our death. Amen.

DAILY RESOLUTION

In the grace of this retreat, I am scheduling a daily meeting time with the Lord. I am determining the most appropriate hour by considering my obligations, and I am deciding on a reasonable length so that I can be faithful to my meeting as time wears on.

THE LIGHT OF THE SAINTS

"Love is so powerful in works that it knows how to profit from everything, from the good and from the bad that it finds in me."[1]

—Thérèse of the Child Jesus, quoting
St. John of the Cross

"He Himself drew me into the fire of living love on which everything converges."[2]

—St. Faustina

1. Thérèse of Lisieux, *The Complete Therese of Lisieux*, trans. Robert J. Edmonson, CJ (Brewster, Mass.: Paraclete Press, 2009), p. 162.

2. Maria Faustina Kowalska, 704.

GUIDE FOR A SECOND PRAYER TIME

Thanks to a regular encounter with God in prayer, everything that makes up my life winds up finding its unity in God.

The demon is the one who divides, who disperses. God is he who gathers up, who unifies. In attaching myself in love to the one true God, I progressively find unity in my life and my person.

I meditate on the text of Sacred Scripture:

"Hear, O Israel: The Lord our God is one Lord; and you shall love the Lord your God with all your heart, and with all your soul, and with all your might. And these words which I command you this day shall be upon your heart" (Deut 6:4–6).

I am taking several minutes to learn by heart this essential text from the Old Testament. I repeat it softly and several times over, with my eyes closed, attentive to each word, letting it permeate me.

I give thanks to God who takes me entirely up into his infinite love.